MARTIAL ARTS IN ACTION

KICKBOXING

MARTIAL ARTS IN ACTION

KICKBOXING

BY GAIL MACK

Marshall Cavendish
Benchmark
New York

With thanks to the Jewish Community Center in Manhattan,
teen kickboxing instructor Louisa Plous,
and her students for their assistance with this book.

Other Marshall Cavendish Offices:
Marshall Cavendish International (Asia) Private Limited, 1 New Industrial Road, Singapore
536196 • Marshall Cavendish International (Thailand) Co Ltd. 253 Asoke, 12th Flr, Sukhumvit
21 Road, Klongtoey Nua, Wattana, Bangkok 10110, Thailand • Marshall Cavendish (Malaysia)
Sdn Bhd, Times Subang, Lot 46, Subang Hi-Tech Industrial Park, Batu Tiga, 40000 Shah Alam,
Selangor Darul Ehsan, Malaysia

Marshall Cavendish is a trademark of Times Publishing Limited

All websites were available and accurate when this book was sent to press.

Library of Congress Cataloging-in-Publication Data
Mack, Gail.
Kickboxing / Gail Mack.
p. cm. — (Martial arts in action)
Includes index.
ISBN 978-0-7614-4936-2 (print)
ISBN 978-1-60870-366-1 (ebook)
1. Kickboxing—Juvenile literature. I. Title.
GV1114.65.M33 2012
796.815—dc22
2010014798

Editor: Peter Mavrikis
Publisher: Michelle Bisson
Art Director: Anahid Hamparian
Series design by Kristen Branch

Photo Research by Candlepants Incorporated

Cover Photo: Keystone/Magali Girardin / AP Images

The photographs in this book are used by permission and through the courtesy of:
Corbis: © IDC/amanaimages, 2; © ROB & SAS, 9; © Nancy Ney, 10; © Hulton-Deutsch Collection, 14; ©
Tom & Dee Ann McCarthy, 24. Shutterstock: 6. Getty Images: Christopher Furlong, 8, 27, 30; Gavin Hellier,
16; Giulio Marcocchi, 21; Liu Jin/AFP, 22; Andrea Pistolesi, 26; Paul Bradbury, 31; White Packert, 33; David
Leahy, 35; Cornelius Poppe, 37; Peter Dazeley, 41; Peter Cade, 42. Art Resource, NY: Réunion des Musées
Nationaux, 12. Alamy Images: © LOOK Die Bildagentur der Fotografen GmbH, 18; © INTERFOTO, 19;
Photos 12, 20; © Glow Asia, 28; © Ingram Publishing, 29; © image100, 38; © Roland Simpson, 40.

Printed in Malaysia
1 3 5 6 4 2

CONTENTS

CHAPTER ONE

KICKBOXING CLASS

AMY ANN WAS A SEVENTH GRADER WHO had just moved to a new school. She did not know anyone, and was very shy about making new friends. She was a little behind in her schoolwork and found it hard to **focus** sometimes. Amy Ann was short for her age, and sometimes people bullied her, making her feel like she could not stand up for herself.

One day, her mom told her about a **kickboxing** class for teens that was starting at the local community center. She and her mother went to talk to the teacher. Amy Ann had taken gymnastics at her old school, so she thought the kickboxing class sounded like fun. The class was held once a week. Seven girls and six boys signed up for it. They learned how to throw different kinds of punches and practiced

YOUNG MARTIAL ARTISTS WAITING FOR A COMPETITION TO BEGIN.

all kinds of kicks using the big punching bags that hung from the ceiling. They also practiced punches and kicks with each other, but they never really hit or kicked their partners. The kickboxers also did exercises to strengthen their bodies. The students learned how to defend themselves by dodging and avoiding punches and kicks with quick reflexes. Because of all the time she spent working with them, Amy Ann became friends with the other students in her kickboxing class.

As the weeks went by, Amy Ann's parents noticed their daughter was changing in many surprising ways. Her attitude toward adults and other teenagers became more respectful. Her grades improved.

STRETCHING EXERCISES HELP THESE YOUNG KICKBOXERS PREPARE FOR THEIR TRAINING.

Amy Ann told them, "Kickboxing practice teaches me how to focus. I know how to pay total attention to what I am learning. I don't do it just at kickboxing—now I focus in school, too, in math class, and English, and other classes. The teachers love that! We have to bring our report cards to kickboxing, so the teacher knows how we are doing, and it's important to her that we do well in school, not just in kickboxing." Amy Ann continued, "Kickboxing helps us set goals for what we want to accomplish. I didn't know how important that is, but I do now."

A KICKBOXING INSTRUCTOR WORKS WITH HIS STUDENTS.

SELF-DEFENSE SKILLS HELP MARTIAL ARTISTS DEVELOP SELF-CONFIDENCE IN MANY AREAS OF THEIR LIVES.

The exercise Amy Ann got in kickboxing class helped her sleep better and stay fit. She also is not as scared of people. She has learned to defend herself by being aware of those around her, sensing if a situation or certain people may be dangerous. Avoiding danger will keep her safe from physical confrontations. But if she had to, she could punch or kick to give her enough time or space to get away from the dangerous situation and to safety.

In school, Amy Ann is self-confident. She is proud of her accomplishments and feels good about who she is and what she is doing. She knows that she can accomplish things if she sets goals and sticks to them. Even if it seems tough, she is willing to try.

CHAPTER TWO
KICKBOXING: OUT OF THE PAST AND INTO THE
THE PRESENT

KICKBOXING IS RECOGNIZED AS ITS own martial art. But it developed from ancient arts. Other martial arts from around the world also feature kicks, punches, and forms of fighting that can still be seen in some kickboxing moves today.

In Europe, more than two thousand years ago, the ancient Greeks held competitions at an international religious festival on the Isthmus of Corinth. The festival honored Poseidon, god of the sea. Among the contests were boxing and wrestling matches. The fighters used all sorts of powerful methods—punching and kicking, choking, throwing, and other moves that would knock down and sometimes kill their opponents. This way of fighting was called **pankration**. It became

THIS ANCIENT GREEK VASE SHOWS TWO YOUNG MEN BOXING.

an Olympic sport in 648 BCE. Some historians believe that today's martial arts developed from this bloodthirsty way of fighting.

MUAY THAI IN THAILAND

Over a thousand years later, another form of boxing called **Muay Thai** developed in Siam, part of which is now called Thailand. Historians believe Muay Thai developed in the fourteenth century, but they cannot be sure about the date because war destroyed many records and other documents.

A MUAY THAI INSTRUCTOR USES PROTECTIVE PADS ON HIS HANDS WHILE TRAINING A KICKBOXER.

Muay Thai began as a form of military combat used by soldiers who carried swords, battle-axes, spears, and crossbows. The soldiers also had a "how-to" manual that showed how to use their weapons. This guide, called the *Chupasart*, also taught the soldiers how to use parts of their bodies as weapons. Martial arts scholars believe that this practice probably started about 1459. Just as today's books are revised and updated, the *Chupasart* was revised and updated when new methods of military combat came along.

Up until about one hundred years ago, Muay Thai was very violent and bloody. Fighters wore gloves soaked in glue and covered with crushed glass or seashells. These sharp bits made every hit more painful for their opponents. Around 1927, the fighters started wearing regular Western-style gloves similar to the ones used today.

Today, Muay Thai is the most popular sport in Thailand. The government sponsors many Muay Thai competitions. There are training camps throughout the country where people learn about the sport. Muay Thai's popularity is growing around the world, especially in England and the United States. Those who follow Muay Thai want to see it become an Olympic sport.

CHINA AND EAST ASIA

Most martial arts scholars see China as the birthplace of many martial arts that developed from ancient hunting skills, tribal wars, military combat skills, and a legacy of bandits, pirates, **militias**, secret societies, and invaders who lived and fought in ancient times.

A monk from India also left his mark on the Chinese martial arts tradition. Legends say that the Indian monk Bodhidharma came to

KICKBOXERS COMPETING IN BANGKOK, THE CAPITAL OF THAILAND.

China from southern India in the sixth century. He brought with him a collection of writings. He wanted to bring his ideas to the monks at the **Shaolin Monastery**, nestled deep in the wilderness of China's Henan Province. Many believe that this famous monk was the one who introduced martial arts and Zen Buddhism to China.

KOREA

Korea has given the world the hugely popular martial art of taekwondo. This form of fighting dates back at least two thousand years. Like other martial arts, it is both a sport and a method of self-defense. It is one of the few martial arts that emphasizes kicking. Taekwondo is based mostly on two ancient arts: *taekkyon*, which emphasizes fast combinations of kicks from unexpected angles, as well as fast **takedowns**, and *subak*, which uses fists. Ancient Korean warriors used subak on the battlefield.

In 1973, the Korean government recognized the World Taekwondo Federation (WTF) as the legitimate governing body of the sport. The first World Championships were held that year. Taekwondo became an Olympic sport, beginning with the 2000 Olympic Games held in Sydney, Australia.

JAPAN

Japan's influence on martial arts goes back to ancient military combat moves and continues today with modern techniques and practices in the form of karate. The legacy of the ancient warriors of Japan includes a code of beliefs and **philosophy** called *Bushido*, which means "the way of the warrior." This ancient code lists seven virtues that are held

Kung Fu and Wushu

Westerners know the Shaolin martial arts as *kung fu*. However, in Chinese, kung fu means "learned skill." To some, any learned skill that you can become good at—from skateboarding to driving to chess—can be described as kung fu. But in China, martial arts are called *wushu*.

SHAOLIN MONKS PRACTICE THE TRADITIONAL CHINESE MARTIAL ARTS.

in high esteem by the warriors: honor, loyalty, courage, benevolence, justice, truth, and politeness.

The methods of fighting empty-handed—without weapons and instead using parts of your arms and legs—began when Japan's government banned the use of weapons with blades in 1876.

SAVATE FROM FRANCE

Savate is similar in many ways to Muay Thai. This form of fighting made its way to France from India and China, through French criminals, soldiers, and sailors who got into fights at the seaports and in saloons, where they kicked their way out. Savate means "old shoe." The term comes from a punishment for lazy soldiers in Napoleon's army. The punishment was kicking the soldier in his backside.

A NINETEENTH-CENTURY MAGAZINE ILLUSTRATION SHOWING A SAVATE MATCH.

UNITED STATES

As the 1970s began, karate had become an international sport that was popular in countries throughout the world. Martial arts had made it into the movies. Famous martial-artist movie stars such as Bruce Lee and Chuck Norris amazed audiences with swift, flying kicks and powerful punches. But in the United States, people were not that impressed by karate matches, because the fighters were not allowed to make contact with their opponents. They had to stop short, seconds before they actually kicked or punched their opponents. The sport was called noncontact karate. Even so, sometimes fighters were injured because they did not wear protective gear and their opponents could not stop in time—the kicks or punches were too swift and powerful. Audiences were used to the fast and furious action of martial arts movies. So to them, noncontact karate seemed boring.

Many martial artists, including Bruce Lee, criticized this "artificial" way of fighting. Then, in 1974, the legendary martial artist Jhoon

BRUCE LEE WAS THE FIRST MARTIAL ARTIST TO BECOME FAMOUS WORLDWIDE.

BENNY URQUIDEZ

Benny Urquidez's nickname is "The Jet." Born in Los Angeles, California, in 1952, he grew up with a mom who wrestled and a dad who was a boxer. His sister, Lilly Rodriguez, was one of the first women kickboxers. At five years old, he competed in "Pee Wee" boxing. By the age of eight, he was studying martial arts and, at fourteen, earned a black belt in karate.

He began his career with noncontact karate. But in 1974, when full-contact karate began in the United States, he switched to that. Over the years, he built an amazing record. By the end of his fighting career, he had fifty-eight wins, no losses, and no ties.

MARTIAL ARTS CHAMPION BENNY "THE JET" URQUIDEZ.

THE SPEED AND INTENSITY OF KICKBOXING HAVE MADE IT A POPULAR SPECTATOR SPORT.

Rhee—the man who had brought taekwondo to the United States—made some changes. He invented new protective equipment for fighters' hands, feet, and shins. This foam-covered equipment was called Safe-T-Chop. The equipment was tested in karate matches, and any injuries to the fighters were not serious. The martial artists could at last have full-contact karate matches.

The name of the sport was eventually changed from full-contact karate to kickboxing. Kickboxing was new to America, but the many different martial arts from which it developed have been around for centuries. Today modern kickboxing competitions are held under the strict rules of national and international kickboxing associations. Audiences now flock to see these spectacular matches, and many are televised.

KICKBOXING BASICS

THERE ARE TWO KINDS OF KICKBOXING: semi-contact, in which the kickboxers may land only light, very controlled blows, and full-contact, in which the kickboxers aim at knocking out their opponents. Kickboxing is a hybrid sport that combines many different moves borrowed from other martial arts. Western kickboxers use different kinds of punches, knee blows, and spectacular leg sweeps—front, side, and **back kicks**. Kickboxing demands power, strength, and stamina, meaning staying power or endurance.

Exercising to build body strength, flexibility, and speed is an essential part of training. Fighters lift weights and practice catching a big, heavy object called a medicine ball. This ball helps fighters practice taking a hit. The kickboxers also kick and punch at big, heavy punching

A KICKBOXER TRAINING.

ALL MARTIAL ARTS REQUIRE GREAT PHYSICAL AGILITY.

bags that hang from the ceiling. These big bags are called heavy bags or banana bags—they are about 6 or 7 feet (1.8 to 2.1 meters) long and weigh 200 pounds (91 kilograms). A smaller "chaser" bag bounces from side to side. Punching bags may be stuffed with cloth or filled with water. Kickboxers spend endless hours building their strength and perfecting their kicks and punches. Like all martial artists, they must learn discipline and control.

Full-contact karate is the most popular style of kickboxing in the United States. The Professional Kickboxers Association (PKA)

MANY YEARS OF TRAINING WILL MAKE THIS YOUNG BOY
AN EXPERT KICKBOXER.

was founded in 1974. The PKA came up with the name full-contact karate, and later, full-contact kickboxing. The PKA set the rules and regulations for fighters and competitions. For example, fighters must punch or kick only above their opponents' waists. A PKA match has twelve two-minute rounds, with a one-minute rest in between each round.

Fighters cannot use elbows or knees to deliver blows, and they must make at least eight kicks per round. They must wear protective gear, including boxing gloves, shin pads, footpads, and groin protectors. Some fighters also wear gear that protects their heads. Mouth guards protect teeth and gums. Without them, teeth could be broken, or fighters might accidentally bite their tongues. Women also wear chest protectors.

Since the PKA was founded, at least nine kickboxing organizations have developed. These include the International Kickboxing Association, the United States Kickboxing Association, United States

A POWERFUL BACK KICK.

Kickboxing Federation, World Kickboxing Association, and the World Kickboxing League. Other organizations have been founded in many other countries.

WHAT TO WEAR

Semi-contact kickboxers usually wear karate clothing—a white shirt, a colored belt, and white long pants that end below the knee, but above the ankle. Full-contact kickboxers may wear T-shirts and long pants. The men may be bare-chested and wear shorts. Women may wear tank tops or T-shirts, and shorts or long pants.

PROTECTIVE GEAR, INCLUDING HELMETS AND GLOVES, HELPS KEEP MARTIAL ARTISTS SAFE.

Female Pioneer: Graciela Casillas

Before 1974, women could not compete in full-contact sports. Kickboxing was the first full-contact sport to open its doors to women. Graciela Casillas was a pioneer of women's kickboxing, though her first martial art was taekwondo. Casillas became a star of full-contact karate, and held the World Karate Association world bantamweight title. Her nickname was "The Goddess." She holds a third-degree black belt in kenpo karate, a self-defense martial art that can overwhelm an opponent with very fast moves in rapid-fire succession. She also holds a third-degree black belt in kodenkan jujitsu.

CHILDREN CAN BEGIN TO STUDY KICKBOXING AT A VERY YOUNG AGE.

THE ART OF KICKING

Some people are more flexible than others. If you are practicing kicks, do not try to do a kick perfectly at the beginning. You need to start slowly and warm up. To avoid injuries, you must be mindful of your knees and hips when you are preparing to execute, or do, a kick. At the beginning of your practice, do not try to kick harder or higher than you can normally kick. You should have patience. As time goes on, you will get more and more flexible and powerful.

One way to improve your skills is to practice standing on one foot while trying to keep your balance. When you kick, your other leg and foot will be your support. You need good balance to be a successful kicker. The more you practice, the steadier you will be. Most kickboxing kicks begin with the fighter lifting his or her knee up to the chest. This move is called **chambering.**

FRONT KICK

One of the simpler kicks to perform is the **front kick**. Raise the knee of the leg you will use so that it is at least parallel with the floor. The knee of your supporting leg should be

A YOUNG WOMAN DEMONSTRATES THE FRONT KICK.

bent and steady, and your supporting foot should point forward. Kick out with your ankle forward and your toes back. The point of contact, or the place that touches your target, should be the ball of your foot.

SIDE KICK

To do a **side kick**, raise the knee of your kicking leg so that it is at least parallel with the floor. The knee of your supporting leg should be bent and steady, and your supporting foot should point sideways. Turn your hips until the thigh of your kicking leg faces the target, and your lead hip is comfortable. Thrust your kicking leg sideways and out, while bending your ankle and pulling your toes back. The point of contact will be the edge of your foot.

FRONT LEG ROUND KICK

To do this, raise the knee of the kicking leg so that it is at least parallel with the floor. The knee of the supporting leg should be bent and steady, and your supporting foot should point sideways. Begin to turn the hip of the kicking leg as you "flick" the leg out in a semicircle. The point of contact is your heel.

REAR LEG ROUNDHOUSE KICK

Chamber the right leg and turn your supporting leg more than 90 degrees to the left and extend your kicking leg. Swing the leg up and out in a semicircle. You can strike the target with your shin, ball of your foot, or instep (the inside edge of your foot). If you use your shin, you will not need to chamber your right leg.

BACK KICK

To do a back kick, turn on the ball of your front foot, so that your body spins 180 degrees. Raise the knee of your kicking leg so that it is at least parallel with the floor. The knee of the supporting leg should be bent and steady, and the supporting foot should point directly backwards. Push the kicking leg out backwards, toward your target. The point of contact is your heel.

THE BACK KICK IS ONE OF THE MOST EFFECTIVE MOVES IN KICKBOXING.

THE ART OF PUNCHING

If you plan to train by punching a heavy bag, you may want to bandage your hands before putting on boxing gloves. Bandaging is used by most boxers to prevent their knuckles from spreading when they punch.

JAB

Your lead, or punching, arm is never fully extended in a **jab**. To perform a jab, raise your shoulder (left or right, depending on which hand you use), keep your chin tucked in, and your elbow protecting your ribs. Strike out with the lead arm to hit your target.

HOOK

This type of punch is thrown from close range, using either your lead or your rear hand. To do this, throw your punching arm out and forward. Raise your elbow and tighten your shoulder and armpit. Hit your target using a horizontal **hook** action. The back of your knuckles should be facing upward.

UPPERCUT

This is another close-range punch. You may want to use this one as a surprise tactic to catch your opponent off-guard. It is one of the most powerful punches you can throw. Using either hand, start from a crouching position and punch upward. Protect your chin—keep it tucked in—and with your other hand protect your ribs and chin.

Uppercuts often result in a knockout, but are considered controversial in kickboxing because the punch snaps the opponent's head back and can cause serious damage to a fighter.

BOTH THIS KICKBOXER AND HIS TRAINER NEED PROTECTIVE GEAR WHEN PRACTICING PUNCHES.

CROSS

This powerful punch is often used together with a jab. When throwing it, you usually aim for your opponent's jaw. Like the uppercut, it can knock out an opponent. To do a **cross**, thrust out your punching arm from one side of your body. The punch should cross an imaginary midline across your body. Throw the punch from a range that is medium or long. When you use a cross, keep your non-punching

BILL "SUPERFOOT" WALLACE

"Superfoot" Wallace earned his nickname from his superfast left leg. He could punch fast, and with that left leg, he could kick just as fast. He was especially good at roundhouse and hook kicks. In 1974, he turned professional and won the Professional Kickboxing Association's middleweight karate championship with a knockout in the second round of the match.

FEMALE KICKBOXERS COMPETING IN THE RING.

hand straight up, with your elbow pointing down to protect your ribs. Keep your fist near—but not touching—your jaw as added protection.

Doing punches correctly takes time and practice. You can practice your punches by using focus mitts with a partner. Your partner wears these protective gloves while you aim for them. Punching these special pads will improve your accuracy, timing, and speed.

Your partner will hold the mitts in different positions for different punches. There are other kinds of equipment, too, that will help you develop the skills you need in kickboxing. With time and work, you will develop the focus, power, speed, timing, and accuracy that you need to excel in kickboxing.

KICKBOXING AND YOU

PICKING THE RIGHT KICKBOXING school or program is important for learning the art. You should not rush into a program or school just because it is near where you live. Do some research and ask around. You can even contact a kickboxing organization for programs they recommend. It is also possible that friends or classmates may know of different kickboxing programs.

When you consider different programs, you need to watch the classes. Watch how the instructors or coaches train their students. Do the students do warm-up exercises before they start their lessons? Some instructors have their students jump rope and do jumping jacks, as well as stretching exercises.

Is the teacher a professional kickboxer? Does she or he have

KICKBOXING REQUIRES COMMITMENT, DISCIPLINE, AND HARD WORK.

CHOOSING THE RIGHT KICKBOXING SCHOOL, AND
THE RIGHT INSTRUCTOR, IS VERY IMPORTANT.

experience with competitions? Does it look like the teacher is showing the proper techniques for punches and kicks? How does the coach deal with students who may be afraid? Does he or she require students to wear protective equipment, and make sure they know how to put it on correctly?

One of the most important parts of choosing a kickboxing program is being comfortable with the class and with the teacher. Many programs will let you take a class or two for free before deciding to commit to a full program.

CARDIO
KICKBOXING

Many people are not interested in being professional, full-contact kickboxers. Instead, they want to practice cardio, or aerobic, kickboxing that is noncontact, exercise-only, body-strengthening kickboxing. Cardio kickboxing is much like dancing. Even that kind of kickboxing will help you get into great condition and make you feel better physically and more confident mentally. Cardio kickboxing classes are offered at most gyms and YMCA programs.

KICKBOXING OFFERS IMPORTANT HEALTH BENEFITS, EVEN FOR PEOPLE WHO ARE NOT VERY INTERESTED IN SELF-DEFENSE.

THIS YOUNG MAN HAS SPENT YEARS DEVELOPING HIS KICKBOXING SKILLS— AND HIS HARD WORK HAS PAID OFF.

THE BENEFITS OF KICKBOXING

When you start training to be a kickboxer, you will be surprised at all the other things you learn. Kickboxing, like the other martial arts, is not just about learning how to kick and punch, and win a fight. It is about much more than that. To be a skilled kickboxer, you will have to work very hard.

There are many physical benefits to kickboxing. Not only will your reflexes improve, but you can build muscles and become stronger. Many people find that kickboxing exercise helps keep their heart and lungs healthy. Combined with a proper diet and other healthy activities, kickboxing can help a person maintain a healthy weight.

Practicing for a long time can help you learn patience and discipline. You will learn to respect your teachers and fellow students. You will also learn to respect yourself for your patience, kindness, courage, and achieving your goals.

Many kickboxing students find that they also improve in school. This is because they have learned how to listen, focus, work hard, and respect others. Martial arts, including kickboxing, teach you not just to think like a warrior, but also to strive for excellence, tolerance, honesty, and integrity. Those values will help you throughout your whole life.

GLOSSARY

back kick—A kick that is usually delivered with the rear leg. The back is turned to the opponent, and contact is made with the heel or full foot.

chamber—A kick's starting move in which the fighter lifts one knee up to the chest.

cross—A powerful punch thrown diagonally across the body, using the fighter's strongest arm.

focus—Strong concentration or attention on a certain subject or activity.

front kick—A kick that is pushed forward and straight out, with contact made at the ball of the foot.

hook—A punch thrown with either hand. The hooking action delivers a powerful punch.

jab—A quick punch using an arm that travels forward in a spiral motion. The jab is usually followed by a stronger punch, such as a hook.

kickboxing—A sport that combines boxing and kicking moves from many different martial arts. Modern kickboxing developed from ancient self-defense and combat techniques used by soldiers, slaves, and others who were not allowed to carry weapons.

kung fu—A term used to describe Chinese martial arts.

militia—A group of citizens who are trained to fight and are called on in times of emergency.

Muay Thai—A style of kickboxing that originated in Thailand.

pankration—An ancient Greek combat sport that combined both boxing and wrestling.

philosophy—A branch of learning that studies the nature of ideas and principles such as truth, wisdom, and reality.

rear leg roundhouse kick—A kick delivered to an opponent's ribs, temples, or jaw, as the kicker turns the back and snaps the rear leg forward.

savate—A French foot-fighting style that most likely came from French colonies in Indo-China during the seventeenth century. It appeared in France when sailors and criminals used it during fights in bars and on the streets.

Shaolin Monastery—Founded in the fifth century, this monastery is known for its association with Chinese martial arts.

side kick—Side kicks can be delivered from the front, rear, or even as a jumping kick.

takedown—Any move or technique that causes an opponent to fall suddenly from a standing position.

uppercut—A punch thrown upward with a bent arm. Kickboxers throw front, rear, and body uppercuts.

wushu—A term used to describe martial arts in China.

FIND OUT MORE

BOOKS

Crudelli, Chris. *The Way of the Warrior: Martial Arts and Fighting Styles from Around the World*. NY: DK Publishing, 2008.

Kaelberer, Angie Peterson. *Kickboxing*. Mankato, MN: Capstone Press, 2006.

Nonnemacher, Klaus. *Kickboxing. Martial Arts*. Milwaukee, WI: Gareth Stevens Publishing, 2005.

Trimble, Aidan. *Kickboxing: Essential Tips, Drills, and Combat Techniques*. Broomall, PA: Mason Crest Publishers, Inc., 2007.

WEBSITES

Martial Arts/Fitness Club
www.kickboxing.com/Styles/

History of Kickboxing
www.angelfire.com/rings/kickboxing/kbhis.html

The Difference Between Boxing and Kickboxing
www.livestrong.com/article/94137-difference-between-boxing-kickboxing/

INDEX

Page numbers in **boldface** are illustrations.

ABOUT THE AUTHOR

Gail Mack is a journalist and author of several books for children. She grew up in Boston, Massachusetts, and currently lives and works in New York City.